REJOINING
JOY

Volume VIII

Sayings

Gerald Young, PhD

Text design & page layout: Kim Monteforte, WeMakeBooks.ca
Cover design: Amy Greenan, amy.greenan@gmail.com

Rejoining Joy Publishing Inc.
Toronto, Ontario, Canada

Volume 8 Sayings:
ISBN 978-1-897478-00-4

www.rejoiningjoy.com

REJOINING JOY: SAYINGS

VOLUME VIII

Gerald Young, Ph.D.
Glendon College
York University

ALSO BY DR. GERALD YOUNG

Books

Young, G., et al. (Eds.)
(2013; in preparation).
*Handbook of Psychological Injury
and Law.* New York: Springer.

Young, G., et al. (Eds.) (2012).
*Psychological Injury and Law:
Introduction.* New York: Springer.

Young, G. (2011). *Development and
Causality: Neo-Piagetian Perspectives.*
New York: Springer.

Young, G. (2010). *Rehabilitation
Psychology [Course Kit].* Toronto,
ON: York University Bookstore.

Young, G., Kane, A. W., & Nicholson,
K. (2007). *Causality in Psychological
Injury: Presenting Evidence in Court.*
New York: Springer.

Young, G., Kane, A. W., & Nicholson,
K. (Eds.) (2006). *Psychological
Knowledge in Court: PTSD, Pain,
and TBI.* New York: Springer.

Young, G. (1997). *Adult Development,
Therapy, and Culture: A Postmodern
Synthesis.* New York: Plenum Press.

Young, G., Segalowitz, S., Corter, C.,
& Trehub, S. (Eds.) (1983). *Manual
Specialization and the Developing
Brain.* New York: Academic Press.

Journals

Young, G. (Founding Editor and
Editor-in-Chief) (2008–)
Psychological Injury and Law.
New York: Springer.

The 2013, 2012, 2010, 2007, and 2006
books are books on psychological
effects of traumatic events, and the like,
in relation to personal injury law. The
2011 and 1997 books are on life span
development. You may also consult the
journal for which I am editor-in-chief,
entitled, *Psychological Injury and Law.* To
see my work in the area of psychological injury and law, consult the web-
sites www.asapil.org and springer.com.
To see my work in the area of self-help
consult www.rejoiningjoy.com.

Rejoining Joy

Gerald Young, Ph.D.

Text design & page layout: Beth Crane, WeMakeBooks.ca
Cover design: Amy Greenan, amy.greenan@gmail.com

978-1-897478-01-1 Rejoining Joy: Essays
978-1-897478-02-8 Rejoining Joy: Destressing
978-1-897478-03-5 Rejoining Joy: Emotions
978-1-897478-04-2 Rejoining Joy: Daily Living
978-1-897478-05-9 Rejoining Joy: Art
978-1-897478-08-0 The Best of Rejoining Joy
978-1-897478-06-6 Rejoining Joy: Workbook of Exercises
978-1-897478-00-4 Rejoining Joy: Sayings

www.rejoiningjoy.com

To my Family and my Clients

REJOINING JOY

A book series in 8 volumes

ABOUT THE AUTHOR

DR. GERALD YOUNG is an Associate Professor Psychology at Glendon College, York University, Toronto, Ontario, Canada. He is also a practicing psychologist dealing with rehabilitation and with counseling. He undertakes research on two major topics. The first is on psychological injury and law [five books]. The second is on child development. His most recent book is entitled: *Cognitive and Affective Parallels in Development: Comparing the Neo-Piagetians Fischer, Case, and Young* (published by Springer SBM, New York). He has written one other book, on the topic of manual and hemisphere specialization. He has received an outstanding research award from his faculty at the university. He is the editor of the leading journal in the area of psychological injury and law (*Psychological Injury and Law*, PIL, springer.com), and is the president of its housing association (ASAPIL, see www.asapil.org).

Dr. Gerald Young has gained the trust of his clients and of his professional colleagues in his professional practice in clinical psychology. He has helped numerous clients over the years; and his reports have been presented to court. As an Associate Professor at York University, he teaches students the courses of Rehabilitation Psychology, and Abnormal Child, Adolescent, Adult, and Advanced Development.

"There is unity in my university teaching, my research, my practice, and the self-help book series. With much passion, I have dedicated my professional life to the area, and the self-help books reflect that passion and the skills that I have learned and developed and want to communicate to the reader."

FOREWORD

Rejoining Joy is a self-help book series on stress, emotions, pain, managing stress, and dealing with a range of daily issues, such as raising a range of daily issues, such as raising children and functioning well at work (see rejoiningjoy.com). The series is not a self-help one in the traditional sense, for it is more about improving our ways of living. It does not simply ask us to be more positive, happy, or better. Rather, it shows the reader how to accomplish these and related goals in a realistic manner. It does not simply give the reader positive statements about the self to learn. Rather, it helps facilitate the reader in *learning new ways of living* by dealing better with the negatives and increasing the positives.

The series is based on figures and accompanying text created by psychologist Dr. Gerald Young in sessions with his clients. The text for each figure is described in one to several paragraphs and, usually, includes a positive message. In his clinical work, Dr. Young encourages people to tell better stories about themselves, to find inner qualities and strengths, to learn destressing skills in order to add to them, and to use appropriately these qualities and strengths in solving problems.

There are eight volumes in the book series.

The first volume presents essays, without accompanying figures for the most part, including an essay on an introduction to psychology, and another on therapy. The next volume, the first with figures and accompanying text, is on stress and destressing. The next two volumes are also in this figure-text format. Specifically, the third volume in the series is on emotions, such as worrying but, also, it includes positive feelings, such as love. The fourth volume deals with diverse topics relating to children, work, change, and so on. The fifth volume has neither essays nor figures and accompanying text, but presents artwork meant to be relaxing. In a sixth book, the reader is provided a self-contained workbook of psychological exercises. In addition, the series includes a seventh book based on excerpts from the best material from books in the series. The eighth book is on sayings for living, loving, and learning. The reader should find them inspirational. They emphasize the major theme of the book series—that when life is difficult, we can still do our best and do it well, and that we choose to find techniques, strategies, and ways of living to help us in this great and empowering task. Another way of describing the major themes of the book is that they involve: Reducing Negatives, Increasing Positives, and Improving Relations and Love. I created over 20 sayings for over 20 themes.

Together, the books are aimed at having the reader not only regain joy but, also, keep it.

Introduction to the Book Series

Dr. Young has written a series of eight self help books. In these self-help books, he shares with you the clinical advice he gives to his clients, most of whom have been in traumatic accidents. A large part of the material in the books consists of graphics and accompanying text. They cover the multiple areas of stress, negative emotions, and life disruptions that follow trauma. There is also an introductory book of essays, a book on art and nature, and a workbook. The series concludes with an excerpted book of the best of the other books. It ends with a book of the sayings, some excerpted from the other books and some newly written for it. The workbook is about *Empowering the Core* and the collection of sayings is about *Living, Learning, and Loving*. Together, the books constitute a series called, *Rejoining Joy*. The title reflects the belief that we can learn to be in charge of our lives and maintain joy even when we might experience traumatic events such as accidents. We can learn to live our life to the fullest, and have a sense that we are in charge no matter what may happen to us, and no matter what our situation or age.

The contents of the books are scientifically-based, yet tailored to each client. The goal in these books is to help people who want to grow, learn from their experiences, and have a more positive and peaceful psychology. The work is based especially on car accident survivors, who come into the office with a whole host of life issues. Therefore, the books covers how to handle stress, how to deal with negative emotions, how to handle injuries and pain, how to cope with death of a loved one, how to handle the many difficulties that emerge in daily life, how to promote positive emotions, and how to improve communication and relationships, deal with children, families, and work, and how to change for the better.

The approach taken is cognitive-behavioral, narrative, interpersonal, and developmental. The books emphasize that ultimately we are responsible for ourselves, but we create that sense of responsibility by active participation in our social relations and daily life, and by actively finding solutions to the problems that may arise in our roles. Even when the worst tragedies happen to us, we can still be in control, learn from the experience and grow, stay ourselves, and be helpful to others. No matter how bad things seem, there is always something that we can direct, adapt to, and live through with inner positivity and peace. Even in the most extreme stress and negative emotions, we can turn to those parts of us that are more positive and peaceful, make them expand, and regain joy. We can learn to emphasize our positives and work with our negatives, to make us better people and to make our future better.

The Book Series Has Taken a Unique Approach

1. The most important point about the book series is that it will be helpful to readers because it presents a wide range of useful strategies, techniques, and ideas for use in daily

life. The book series is not just for people who are undergoing stress, whether through great tragedies such as serious accidents or in the hassles of daily life. The counseling given in the book series also is useful to prevent stresses from growing out of hand, to head off bad habits, and to promote good habits. We all can develop control in our lives and prosper psychologically in our daily activities. There are eight books in the series and it is comprehensive in the topics discussed and the education and instructions given.

2. In addition, the book series reflects an integration of my practice, teaching, and research, yet stays at the level of my clients and the general reader. In an article written in 2008 for the journal *Psychological Injury and Law*, I describe the psychotherapeutic encounter, and argue that it should deal with the whole person, through 10 critical areas, as well as through family counseling and related interventions, if necessary. This model is an integrative one that has guided the present book series, leading me to organize many common psychotherapeutic techniques into a holistic model. It allows me to keep the client in focus in therapy, and facilitate their self-growth, inner peace, and relations with others in their daily lives.

3. The majority of the books use visual graphics with accompanying text. In the heart of the book series, there are 30 such chapters spread over three books. The books are unique in the amount of graphics and in their use as central organizers, with text written solely to explain them. That is, for each visual, usually there is a paragraph or page-long description. For any one chapter, together the graphics cover the major themes important for it. For the excerpted book, the author took material from each of these 30 chapters, in particular, as well as some introductory essays and some art on nature, as described below. In addition, he put in select sayings written for the margins, as described below.

4. The book of introductory essays includes essays that explain psychology and explain psychotherapy. The author wrote these essays instead of using cumbersome footnotes or endnotes. Almost all key words in the visual graphics and their accompanying text are explained in the essays. Other essays are more motivational and inspirational. Finally, there are those that explain development very well, and they are based on my professional publications. This book concludes with a few poems.

5. The art and nature book is a "green" one, for it encourages readers to respect and love the planet and its animals. The art consists of simple line drawings, illustrating that any one can undertake art, and at any age. Also, the themes are peaceful, motivational, and inspirational, such as ones on families, flowers, dancing figures, and art based on a visit to the holy land.

6. The workbook consists solely of workbook exercises, each having a brief introductory text. Most exercises and their introductions fit on one page. Each exercise consists of two questions, asking for up to five possible answers, or at least things to think about. Other workbooks use more text for each exercise, so there are fewer exercises in other books than in the present workbook. Each of the exercises is aimed at creating a sense that one can succeed in taking charge of life's difficulties. The workbook was written so that it can stand alone, and be read without reading any other book in the series.

7. The book of sayings is a collection of sayings used as margin material, but it turned out important in its own right. For the most part, other collections of sayings involve those not written by the authors, but by famous writers and public figures. Because the sayings are tied to the book series, all of them are psychological in nature, which is unlike the case for other books of sayings. The reader will find the sayings are consistent with the major themes of the book, and therefore reasoned, motivating, inspiring, and promoting positives while helping to control negatives.

Who Needs to Read the Book Series?

1. Anyone who has confronted any kind of stress, not just those coming from accidents, should read the book series.
2. Anyone who wants to learn how to handle effectively stress, negative emotions, and bad habits will profit from the book series.
3. Anyone who needs advice on communication, relationships, love, children, teenagers, families, work, and taking responsibility of any kind will keep coming back to the series.

In short, the book series will be useful for almost anyone. Moreover, its attractive visual and workbook format makes for easy reading and good learning.

People of all ages will find the book series interesting and informative, from teenagers to the elderly. Some of the graphics and workbook exercises might seem more appropriate for young people and others for adults. However, readers of all ages, whether they are young or young at heart, will find the book to their liking.

In addition, because the graphics have been made in session and because the workbook is oriented to clients, both treating mental health professionals and their patients should find the book series valuable.

AUDIENCE

Market

The book series was written starting with *clients* right in their sessions. I would make for them the therapeutic visualizations that I have described in order to illustrate what I wanted them to learn and to apply in their destressing and regaining joy. However, the book series is not just aimed at clines in need of mental health services. It aims, as well, for the self-help and self-healing *market, in general.* Many people need and seek simple techniques to use in their attempts to distress and regain joy, and they also seek books that further their sense of meaning and fulfillment, inspire them to change, and facilitate their growth. Therefore, the book series can be of great help to the general reader, given its motivational, inspirational, and reflective contents.

Because of its contents and the way it is written, *psychologists* and other mental health professionals will also find that the book series can be helpful in their practice. The contents of the books can be used effectively with their clients, just like I have used them with mine. For example, psychologists can use the therapeutic visual figures and their associated text to make crucial points in session. The sayings and art can be used to motivate and inspire. The essays can help flesh out therapeutic work, both in terms of facilitating reflection and for giving clients at-home reading assignments.

The advantage of my approach lies in its inclusive nature. I cover so many themes, with one chapter usually per theme. Within each chapter from the three books in the book series that have figures and matching text, there are at least 10 figures. Some are meant to present the same or similar information in different ways. However, most are quite distinct from the others. Because there are about 500 figures in the book series, and they cover a full range of topics, the mental health professional can select from much choice in the material covered by the books for the particular needs presented by clients in sessions. The therapist using my book series can design individually tailored groups of readings and figures for clients to consult.

REJOINING JOY: DESTRESSING

Stress infiltrates every aspect of our life. So can destressing and joy.

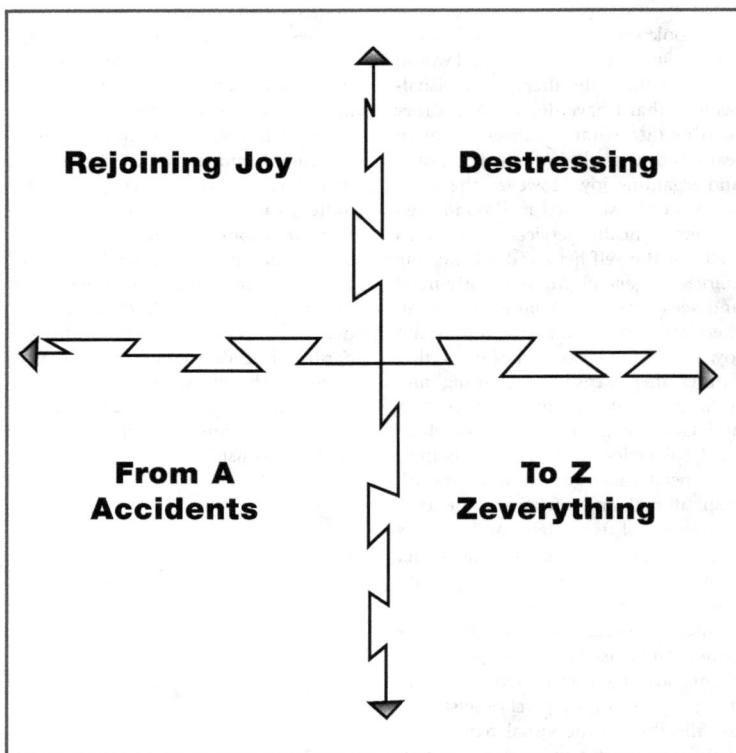

Rejoining Joy

Destressing

**From A
Accidents**

**To Z
Zeverything**

BOOK SERIES CONTENTS

Volume Descriptions

The first volume in the book series presents in a straightforward manner essays introducing psychology and how to live life more happily and effectively. The essays are meant to cover the basic topics presented in the remaining books, and they include pertinent definitions and explanations of concepts, although the reader does not have to read these essays before reading the other books. The topics in the first set of essays range from what are the fundamentals in psychology, to how to deal with stress, to how cognitive behavioral therapy works. The second set of essays is more literary in the first part and more scholarly in the second. The essays range from short ones that are more inspirational and motivational, to ones on change and on stages in development and their implications. Key themes relate to growth and responsibility.

The second volume is on destressing. This volume marks the beginning of the major use of therapeutic figures. In this volume, I explain basic concepts about stress and I explain behavioral techniques on how to distress. I emphasize various cognitive techniques, such as keeping our hope, optimism, and positive attitude. We learn that when confronted with stress, we have options in our behavior and we can be in control. I go on to explain that having some stress can be growth promoting and that we can learn to live effectively

with it. This first book in the series concludes with a chapter on recovering—stress is a start and dealing with it is our goal.

The third volume of the book series deals with negative emotions, such as worry and sadness, and specific emotional problems, such as drinking or dealing with pain. The volume moves from these negative and most basic emotions to positive ones, for it concludes with chapters on love and motivation, in particular. The main theme of this volume is that we can use emotions to our advantage, that emotions color all our activities, and that we can control. Them when they are negative. This third book in the book series concludes with a chapter on rewriting the stories that we tell about ourselves so that they are more positive.

The fourth volume in the book series is about improving the quality of our daily living. It deals with more complex topics, such as the self, communication, handling children and adolescents, coping with change, and managing work and family life. It includes a chapter on inspiration. It terminates with a description of major points of view in psychology, including the biopsychosocial perspective. This reflects the integrative effort that I have taken in writing the book series. To better understand our psychology, we need to look both inside and around us, both at our bodies and our mind, both at our thoughts and our emotions, and both our bad habits and good ones. We all have core positives waiting to grow.

The fifth volume presents two-dimensional artistic line drawings intended to relax and inspire. Many of the drawings are about nature and animals. Many are about people and family. I do these drawings quickly, illustrating that, with a single line or a series of lines, we can both express ourselves and relax in doing so. The accompanying text for this book emphasizes the role that we all have to play in helping nature survive. I added text related to nature and our need to protect and preserve it. By acting to save the planet, its habitats, its animals, and its plants, we engage in the best forms of destressing.

Book six of the book series represents its crowning achievement. It consists of excerpts of the best material, especially from books III, IV, and V of the first five books in the series. I selected those figures and accompanying text that provide the clearest description of the book series' major messages and its best therapeutic self-help skills. The excerpted book offers a concise presentation of the book series contents, allowing the reader to consult the complete series for more in-depth reading.

Book seven presents workbook exercises that have the reader review and reflect on the contents of Books III, IV, and V of the book series. The exercises emphasize empowering our inner positive psychological core and good habits, or strengths and advantages, while helping readers toward altering negatives, bad habits, and so forth. Each of the exercises begins with an introduc-

tory paragraph, so that the reader can read the book by itself, without reference to other books.

The last volume of the book series presents inspirational sayings for living, loving, and learning. The sayings were written based on Dr. Young's work with his clients. They offer a basis for rejoining joy and gaining in life. The third through fifth book of the series concern stress, emotions, and daily living, and there are 10 chapters in each book. For each chapter, there are about 50–100 sayings and bolded sentences that are like sayings. They cover topics such as increasing positives, ensuring success, and improving relationships. There are over 20 topics related to destressing, emotions, and daily living, including at work and with family. There are over 20 sayings per topic. They will motivate, inspire, and help to promote good habits while helping to inhibit negative ones.

What the Book Series is NOT.

To better differentiate how this book series is different from other books similar to them the market, we need to know what the book series is not.

1. The book series is not on one particular topic, such as how to handle stress, depression, or pain, because it covers all these matters. Dr. Young, in his sessions with clients, deals with the full range of issues that come up after accidents and in life.

2. The book series does not give simplistic answers on how to cure or how to deal with all critical problems

that people face because there aren't any such simplistic answers, despite what some people or authors might preach. Books that simplify by giving catchy titles and cute phrases may inspire for the moment, but they do not create long-lasting helpful effects. The approach in the present book series is to not only inspire and teach, but also to have readers learn and apply the strategies in the series, and therefore improve their ways of living.

3. The book series is not a complex scientific explanation of psychology and its therapies. There are not a lot of theoretical explanation, references to the literature, and footnotes. Dr. Young has written scientific books and articles on therapy, but the goal of the present book series is practical and it is aimed at the mass market. The book series speaks to the reader at the level of the reader and gives a bibliography that the reader can consult for further information. Therefore, the book is balanced by being not too simple yet not too complex.

4. The book series is not simply text, because it includes many visuals. For each visual, there is usually an associated paragraph or page, and the visual and the text should be examined together.

5. The book series is not dry and humorless. To the contrary, it includes humor when necessary, it includes some catchy sayings, and there is much to excite the imagination.

6. The book series is not another self-help book project that will not help people. We are coming to understand that self-help books have temporary effects and even some harmful ones. For example, by painting everything rosy or minimizing the difficulties in dealing with problems, other self-help books may overlook the serious problems people have in dealing with stress. Or, they may give very simple solutions that can only work in some situations, but lead to difficulties in others; so in the end, they limit the person and have opposite effects to those intended. The present book series is more realistic, never promising too much. However, it always offers good ideas and strategies, it motivates, and it always gives hope. **Life is a Lesson and we are both its teacher and student.**

7. The book series is not just for accident survivors. Indeed, it will be helpful for most people who want to learn how to handle stress of any kind, and regain joy. Also, it will be helpful to any one wishing to grow and transform for the better. Often, psychology is considered as a discipline that deals with helping people with their problems. The approach of the present book series goes beyond this, because psychology can help all of us all, no matter what out age, to learn to improve our psychological wellness, positivity, quality of life, ways of living, and joy in living.

PREFACE

The title of this book series includes the phrase, "Rejoining Joy." When we experience stress, we do the best that we can to get through it. We try to regain joy, and we use various destressing techniques, perhaps some like the techniques in this series. Rejoining joy is the goal so that we can get on with our lives and live it in enriching, productive ways. "A healthy way of living" is an important means to attain joy.

However, destressing is not a list of techniques mechanically applied. It is essential to want to destress and go beyond our repertoire of learned destressing techniques. People can learn to minimize or take away their present stress. It is just as important to learn that destressing is an ongoing process. When we go beyond the techniques used and see the whole picture, it becomes easier to deal with future stress.

The book series *Rejoining Joy* is divided into eight volumes. They cover a diversity of topics related to destressing, *a)* the nature of stress and how to best deal with it, *b)* the topic of emotions, such as worry, anger, motivation, and love, and *c)* topics relevant to daily life, such as communication, children, and work. The series does not try to cover every area relevant to destressing, nor does it attempt to be exhaustive. In order for readers to complete their knowledge and appreciation of the available destressing techniques in the field, they should consult other relevant self-help

books, their family physicians, and, if necessary, mental health professionals, such as psychologists.

The *Rejoining Joy* book series is unique because it makes extensive use of visualizations, illustrations, drawings, figures, diagrams, graphs, charts, tables, and so on. In the book series, for the most part, I refer to them as "figures." The advantage of using the visual modality is that it captures simply the message that is being communicated. Moreover, visualizations are like verbal metaphors. They suggest, inspire, make people think, and so on, and often avoid direct instruction. Thus, they can function as powerful therapeutic tools. Within each chapter, the figures are loosely organized. It is not necessary that they be read in sequence from first to last. Each figure is meant to be a self-contained unit. Although there is accompanying text, each figure can be understood without reference to it. Similarly, the text can be read and understood without reference to any associated figure. Therefore, the reader can read the text on its own without reference to the figures, or can flip through the figures without reference to the text, or go back and forth between them.

One result of this format is that, at times, there are repetitions. For example, the idea of having a positive attitude is a common theme in the book series; instead of seeing this repetition as a drawback, we can see it as positive because it allows for the accentuation of important themes. The reader should note that, although the focus of the book series is on figures, graphs, and so on , such visualizations have their time and place. For example, if using the book series, the therapist should not simply rely on visualizations. It is important to see each client as an individual with particular problems in particular stressful situations and, only when it is appropriate, should visualizations be used.

In our streams of consciousness, we find not only words and ideas but, also, visual images, both of what happened in the past and what can happen in the future. Therapists can use more effectively the human penchant to visualize. Often, the visual modality is neglected in our thinking process regarding more positive stories that we can tell to ourselves and to others. The current book series aims to rectify this oversight through its many therapeutic visualizations. Narratives need not be verbal alone.

Dream Dance

The joy of music, rhythm, and dance invigorates life and provides the best source of destressing. We are connected in the smooth flow of coordinated, undulating bodies and the powerful chant of multitudes singing. Music and dance empower both individual and group. We sing in unison in choirs, or dance together to the trance of drumbeats. Or, we simply absorb the enchanting melodies that we hear at symphonies, at concerts, on the radio, or from our electronic devises. We listen to music as we fall asleep and it carries into the reverie of our dreams. **Music is to life, as life is to life.**

ACKNOWLEDGMENTS

The book series on Rejoining Joy owes much to my teachers, some of the best of whom have been my clients. It is their stories that have inspired me. Often, it is their ideas and solutions that I put into written and visual form. Often, they are like psychologists, and I simply facilitate the dialogue that they are having in their own minds about which course of action to follow, which advice to accept, and so on.

Another special set of teachers has involved my family, including my mother (Rosalind) and my late father (Samuel), my wife (Lelia) and our children (Carina, Joy, Victoria). They have been great teachers about children and parenting, as has been our first grandchilden, David and Osher. In turning to rehabilitation psychology, I owe much to Stephen Swallow, who was an excellent supervisor and mentor. Other important teachers whom I have had in my student and professional life have included: Jim Alcock, John Crozier, Thérèse Gouin Décarie, Neville Doxey, Michael Lewis, Edward Meade, Ronald Melzack, Gert Morgenstern, Marvin Simner, and Peter H. Wolff. To all these people, I say a hardy THANK YOU.

I would like to thank the following people who have helped put together the book series. Orden Braham of epromotions completed the computer graphics following the hand written figures that I gave him, and he turned them into the professional quality so clearly evident. Beth Crane of WeMakeBooks.ca worked diligently setting up the pages in their attractive format and provided timely advice, as well. Moreover, she greatly improved on the organization of the contents of the figures. Kim Monteforte set up the pages for the sayings book. Also Cindy Cake expertly put together the child alphabet book, which has been placed on the website for the book series (rejoiningjoy.com). Finally, Heidy Lawrance contributed to the last phases of preparing the book series for the website. The website itself is an excellent one, thanks to her work and that of Nathan Lawrance and Donna Lam, who worked so creatively on it.

Carina Young Rock had worked arduously on the first draft of some of the graphics, and Arthur Demerjian has helped her in this regard. More important, Carina Young Rock has provided photographs for the book series, the excellent quality of which is noticeable. These are, first, from the holy land and its nature preserves. Also, she took pictures in New York State. Brian Rock has added wonderful pictures of Switzerland. Joy Young provided the pictures of Toronto. Not to be left out, I added pictures from my visits to the San Francisco area and the Phoenix area (where conferences took place). Carina Young Rock and Joy Young have contributed some artwork to the series (Carina: the introductory art to Volume IV; Joy:

Figures 29.11 and the loon in Northern Bird in Volume V). They collaborated in writing the essay entitled, "Harmony."

Polly's parents have given kind permission for me to reproduce her epitaph (text for Figure 29.11) and the Foreword to the sayings book.

Editors and proofreaders must have patience, and, and I give Joy Young, Carina Young, Victoria Young, Catherine Leek, and Shayna Buhler many thanks. Jessica Chan and Darcy Winkler provided pertinent advice. Don Bastian provided incisive feedback from an editor's perspective that led to improvements in the final draft. Finally, a colleague, Andrew Kane, provided feedback on the essay, "On Psychology," demonstrating his effective writing skills.

Joy Young and Candice Rubinstein undertook the noble effort of struggling through my handwriting to type the manuscript. They had help from Regina Altarkovsky, Jessie Amaral, Melissa Canastraro, Kaitlyn Chambers, Jessica Chan, Joyce Chan, Aline Demerjian, Bonnie Donaldson, Hilary Downes, Paula Druzga, Ilana Gorodezky, Michelle Greisman, Urszula Jasiowka, Natalie Kardasopoulos, Ko Khaira, Vanessa Kissoon-Singh, Simone McMillan, Kathy Raufi, and Darcy Winkler.

I wish to thank Plenum Publishing Company (now called Springer Science & Business Media) for their kind permission to use full or adapted versions of material from my 1997 book, entitled *Adult Development, Therapy, and Culture: A Postmodern Synthesis*. The material forms the basis of the following figures in this series: E2-2, E2-3, E2-4, 7.5, 18.4, 26.5, 28.10, and 29.9. The poem entitled "A Healing Poem" is repro-duced from that book, as is the essay "Reflections for Adults in Transition or Crisis." The art piece introducing Volume IV is taken from the cover of the Plenum book. Springer gave kind permission to take excerpts from chapters in my 2006 and 2007 books for the appendix in the book of essays. The first appendix is constituted by an excerpted, condensed version of a chapter by Young and Yehuda (2006). The second appendix is mostly constituted by excerpts from a chapter by Young, Kane, and Nicholson (2007), and by excerpts from an undergraduate BA research thesis by Janice Dias, written under my supervision, and published with permission by the authors. Parts of the essay entitled "Rehabilitation Psychology" are based on an article that I published in 2008 in the Springer journal that I edit, *Psychological Injury and Law*. Springer also gave permission to use material from my book in press for a section of the introductory essay on psychology and for two figures.

Many thanks to Mark Biernacki, LLB, of the law firm Smart and Biggar, for securing copyright and intellectual property rights for the book series and the website.

If you would like to order material related to *Rejoining Joy*, such as the artwork or the photographs, kindly visit **www.regainingjoy.com**.

Gerald Young, Ph.D.
Department of Psychology
Glendon College, York University
Toronto, Ontario, Canada
February, 2011

SUGGESTED PROFESSIONAL READINGS

There are many books available for the interested reader. Robert Sapolsky (2004) has written an excellent trade book on the topic of stress. Boenisch and Haney (2004) present a fine book with ways of dealing with stress. In terms of dealing with the psychological trauma after an accident, the reader should consult Hickling and Blanchard (2006). A more academic description of stress can be found in Lehrer, Woolfolk, and Sime (2007). Pain management techniques are described very well in Turk and Winter (2006) and in Thorn (2004). The psychology textbooks that I use to teach my courses at the university have provided me with an excellent fund of knowledge (Arnett; DeHart and colleagues; Wicks-Nelson and Israel). For my own work, the reader is referred to Young (1997), Young (2007), and Young and colleagues (2006, 2007). For those interested in original academic journal articles on stress and destressing, you may consult: *Anxiety, Stress, and Coping; International Journal of Stress Management; Journal of Psychological Trauma; Journal of Traumatic Stress; Work and Stress, Traumatology, Journal of Child & Adolescent Trauma,* and *Psychological Traumas: Theory, Research, Practice, and Policy.*

Arnett, J. J. (2007). *Adolescence and Emerging Adulthood: A Cultural Approach* (3rd ed.). Upper Saddle River, NJ: Pearson.

Boenisch, E., & Haney, C. M. (2004). *The Stress Owner's Manual: Meaning, Balance, & Health in Your Life* (2nd Ed.). Atascadero, CA: Impact.

DeHart, G. B., Sroufe, L. A., & Cooper, R. G. (2004). *Child Development: Its Nature and Course* (6th ed.). Boston: McGraw Hill.

Lehrer, P. M., Woolfolk, R. L., & Sime, W. E. (2007). *Principles and Practice of Stress Management* (3rd ed.). New York: Guilford Press.

Hickling, E. J., & Blanchard, E. B. (2006). *Overcoming the Trauma of Your Motor Vehicle Accident: A Cognitive-Behavioral Treatment Program Workbook.* New York: Oxford University Press.

Sapolsky, R. M. (2004). *Why Zebras Don't Get Ulcers: Guide to Stress, Stress-Related Disease, and Coping* (3rd ed.). New York: Freeman.

Thorn, B. E. (2004). *Cognitive Therapy for Chronic Pain: A Step-by-Step Guide.* New York: Guilford.

Turk, D. C., & Winter, F. (2006). *The Pain Survival Guide: How to Reclaim Your Life.* Washington, DC: American Psychological Association.

Wicks-Nelson, R., & Israel, A. C. (2009). *Behavior Disorders of Childhood.* (7th ed.). Upper Saddle River, NJ: Pearson.

SUGGESTED SELF-HELP READINGS

In a certain sense, there is no competition for this book series because it is unique in the ways described. In another sense, the other self-help books that are presented below do very well and promise to continue to do well. Given that the present book series is unique compared to them, it is complementary to the others, and reader will find it an excellent addition to their self-help book library. Or, for young people, it could be a great way to start in self-help, learn psychology, or otherwise be inspired, learn, and grow. In the following, we review some recent books on the topic that are somewhat related to the present book series. By comparing them to the present book series, we illustrate not that the present book series is better, but that the field is ripe for another self-help book in psychology having the series positive characteristics, as described in the above.

A. **The first group of competitors in the field that I examine consists of workbooks.**

1. The first one is by Martha Davis, Elizabeth R. Eshelman, and Matthew Mckay Eliz called, *The relaxation & stress reduction workbook*. It follows the traditional model of workbooks, with a lot of text and exercises given throughout the chapters. The workbook in the present book series differs from it by having most of the exercises being one page in length, so that there are hundreds of them in the book. Each of mine has a brief introductory text that can stand alone, is interesting to read, and relates to a major theme in the other book in the series. Then, each introductory text is followed by two questions. Both questions are aimed at having the reader learn how to handle the issue presented in the exercise and feel confident in doing so.

2. The book by Glenn R. Schiraldi, *The post traumatic stress disorder sourcebook*, follows the same model. It covers many common therapeutic techniques to help clients deal with their traumas. It also covers the effects of trauma on many aspects of daily life. The present book series covers the material in Schiraldi, but in a more concise way, allowing coverage of many other topics.

3. The next book is *Mind over mood*, by Dennis Greenberger and Christine A. Padesky. It is a workbook that deals with cognitive-behavioral therapy, for example, for depression. Many of the workbook exercises deal with standard cognitive-behavioral techniques. In comparison, in my book series, although it is based on a cognitive-behavioral approach, it is not strictly on that approach. It is more expansive in how it deals with problems, yet nevertheless it is grounded in the cognitive-behavioral approach.

4. The next book is by Margaret A. Caudill and it is called, *Managing pain before it manages you*. The title shows a similarity with the present approach because a lot of what is done in the present book series is aimed at helping people manage their problems. The Caudill workbook is written in the standard workbook format, with a lot of text and exercises. It includes chapters on communication and problem solving. The comments for this book are similar to those of the others—it is well done but it deals with a limited range of difficulties that people confront after trauma and in their daily lives.

5. The same can be said for the workbook by Martin M. Anthony and Richard P. Swinson, called, *The shyness and social anxiety workbook*. Comparative analysis reveals that most likely at the scientific level, this workbook is the best one. It emphasizes that we are the experts and it intends that we generalize from what we learn so that we can deal with future difficult social situations. Once more, it is noted that the present book series covers a broader range of material, and is complementary to this one.

6. *Mindstorms* is a book written by John W. Cassidy, and it is a guide for families living with traumatic brain injury. It gives suggestions to families and patients, but it is not a workbook, *per se*. The present book series does not focus on traumatic brain injury, but it can help patients and families dealing with the stress, emotional upset, and effects on daily living that accompany traumatic brain injury.

To conclude, all these workbooks that I have reviewed are complementary to my own, but, given its advantages, mine will gain a fair share of the market and prosper in sales.

B. **The second set of competitor books that are examined are not workbooks, but are more general ones, mostly with text, rather than exercises.**

1. The first one is by Barbara L. Fredrickson, called, *Positivity*. Positive psychology is a recent, fast-developing field, and Dr. Fredrickson builds on her concept of "broaden and build" to construct a helpful book. In her book, she ends up with suggestions for increasing positivity and flourishing, and offers a helpful toolkit of ideas. She does not have workbook exercises and does not use visuals. Given this contrast, the present book series is different and unique. At the same time, although it is not called a book directly on positive psychology, it is steeped in this approach.

2. The second book is by Stephanie McClellan and Beth Hamilton, who have written a book called, *So stressed*. It explains very well from a scientific basis the negative effects of stress on our body and on our psychology. It develops a stress detox program and indi-

cates how we can build resilience and regain peace of mind. There are a lot of similarities in the present approach in dealing with these matters, although the present book series is medical than them and deal with many more issues than just handling stress. There are also the other differences described in the above that make the present book series special.

3. James Hollis wrote a book on, *What matters most*. In a certain sense, my own book deals with similar issues. He considers love and living fully, wisdom and spirituality, adopting new ways of living, finding meaning, and creating our own paths and journeys. The present book series deals with these topics, as well, as it is not simply just about handling stress and emotions on a momentary level. It is also about living a full life, and it reflects my basic philosophy that life is about re-responsibility or taking on responsibilities that make sense to us and about continually re-dedicating ourselves to these responsibilities. Our responsibilities might include raising children with love, living with our partners in love, and studying and working with dedication and application.

4. Another book about daily living and change has been written by David Posen, called, *Always change a losing game*. It deals with making the right choices, avoiding traps, strengthening beliefs, and so on. As with these other books reviewed in this section, it consists mostly text. Not only does the present book series deal with the themes in this book, it also deals with them in the unique ways indicated.

5. Ronald D. Siegel has written a book on the very influential approach of mindfulness, called, *The mindfulness solution*. Mindfulness is a kind of meditation that is simple to use and apply. As explained by Siegel, mindfulness can help deal with anxiety, depression, pain, and stress. Also, the book discusses areas of daily living, such as romance and parenting. Mindfulness can help us break bad habits, change, and grow.

The reader will notice that the present book series deals with all of these, although it does not refer to techniques as mindfulness, *per se*. Rather than teach one technique, the book series offers an array of choices to the reader and they can combine them in ways that are effective for them, while adding to them other coping resources. The approach of the author to psychotherapy and counseling is not about technique. Nor is it about theory. Rather, the present book series is about learning about oneself and growing, on the one hand, and about genuinely meeting the person in context at the individual level, on the other hand.

6. Finally, there are self-help books with catchy titles and contents, such as written by Leil Lowndes, on *How to instantly connect with anyone*. The reader will appreciate that the book series includes

hundreds of sayings in the margins of the text pages, and has gathered them into a book fully dedicated to presenting them. In addition, the present book series has put in bold font hundreds of sentences in the text that are catchy and that are worthy of emphasis. However, the approach of the author in writing these sayings and sentences has been to be educational and instructional, and not only wise, humorous, inspiring, and realistic. Dr. Young wants the reader to remember and act on the sayings. However, more important, he would especially like the reader to remember specific behavioral and cognitive techniques and other strategies that have proven through psychological and scientific bases to lead to constructive change in the ways of living.

BIBLIOGRAPHY

Anthony, M. M., & Swinson, R. P. (2nd Ed.) (2008). *The Shyness And Social Anxiety Workbook*. Oakland, CA: New Harbinger.

Cassidy, J. W. (2009). *Mindstorms: The Complete Guide For Families Living With Traumatic Brain Injury*. Cambridge, MA: Da Capo Press.

Caudill, M. A. (3rd Ed.) (2009). *Managing Pain Before It Manages You: Change How You Feel By Changing The Way You Think*. New York: Guilford Press.

Davis, M., Eshelman, E. R., & McKay, M. (6th Ed.) (2008). *The Relaxation & Stress Reduction Workbook*. Oakland, CA: New Harbinger.

Fredrickson, B. L. (2009). *Positivity*. New York: Crown.

Greenberger, D., & Padesky, C. A. (1995). *Mind Over Mood*. New York: Guilford Press.

Hollis, J. (2009). *What Matters Most: Living A More Considered Life*. New York: Gotham Books.

Lowndes, L. (2009). *How To Instantly Connect With Anyone*. New York: McGraw Hill.

McClellan, S., & Hamilton, B. (2010). *The Ultimate Stress Relief Plan For Women: So Stressed*. New York: Free Press.

Posen, D. (2009). *Always Change A Losing Game: Winning Strategies For Work, For Home, And For Your Health*. Toronto, ON: Key Porter Books.

Schiraldi, G. R. (2nd Ed.) (2009). *The Post Traumatic Stress Disorder Sourcebook*. New York: McGraw Hill.

Siegel, R. D. (2010). *The Mindfulness Solution: Everyday Practices For Everyday Problems*. New York: Guildford Press.

CONCLUSION

Readers should note that the book series may not apply fully to them. Some parts might strike home, while others may be too advanced or may not address personal situations. On the other hand, readers may find that some parts have raised points that they have avoided. A good response would be to say to oneself, "I didn't realize that this book series could help me with this situation. I will keep going in my reading to help me with it."

Throughout the book series, I use some humour, irony, and other means of inducing smiles or laughter. When clients first enter my office, the use of humour is not appropriate. However, humour can help as sessions proceed, as long as it is used sensitively for helping clients move forward.

Note that in this series, I have protected the confidentiality of my clients. In this regard, at the few points when I do refer to particular clients or case studies, their background characteristics, situations, and issues have been altered in order to protect their anonymity.

In summary, I have written a self-help book series with unique features. There are eight books in the series, and the total pages across the books that are available to the reader number almost 2,000 pages. The book series should be appealing to the general reader, as well as mental health professionals and their patients. It will have a long shelf life, so readers should keep it on their reading list for years to come, and consult the full series, available at www.rejoiningjoy.com. We look forward to your feedback.

From Science to Practice and from Practice to Science

[Summary of an article published in the *Trauma Division Newsletter* of the American Psychological Association, 2009]

Evidence-based practice concerns application of sound scientific empirical investigation of psychological interventions to the treatment of patients. Moreover, it includes the capacity to engage in critical thinking, using scientific principles, in analyzing the quality of the research and in applying it to the patient being treated. Evidence-based practice adjusts to the wide individual variations in the population and the limits of the research.

Ideally, psychotherapy is a dynamic encounter of the therapist and patient, as they strive together to establish pathways to empowerment and improvement in the patient. Psychologists are trained in according to schools of thought, but often prefer eclectic and individualized approaches. We treat people for their symptoms rather than treating them for how they fit into schools of thought and learned techniques.

For a scientifically informed approach to psychotherapy published in the journal, see: Young, G. (2008). Psychotherapy for psychological injury: A biopsychosocial and forensic perspective. Psychological Injury and Law, 1 (4), 287-310. (www.asapil.org)

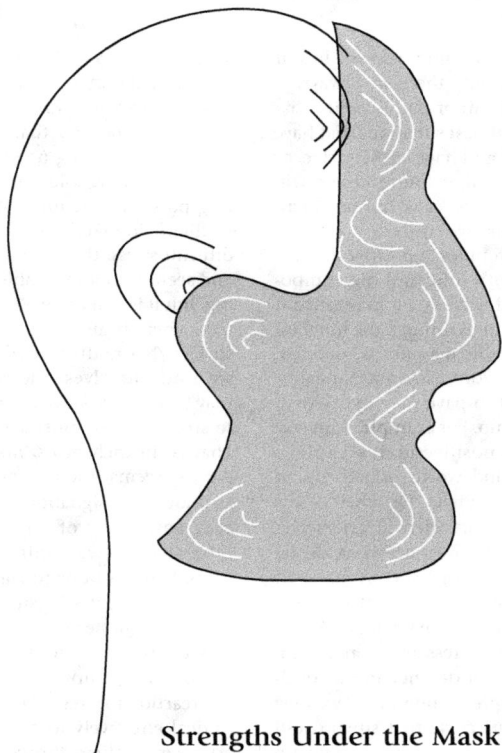

Strengths Under the Mask

Each of us has a unique set of core strengths that make us special. Each of us has weaknesses that can be improved by self-exploration, social support, and good advice. What others see in us is not a measure of what we know to be true of ourselves. At the same time, we may be confused about who we are, what are our strengths and virtues, and where we want to go and grow. **When times are difficult, we need to know that we have positive psychological anchors that can help us stabilize, preparing constructive change.** These can be found by being vigilant to our depths. By seeking inside, we will find constructive paths to the outside. By taking constructive paths on the outside, our inside anchors will grow.

VOLUME I — INTRODUCTION FOR ESSAYS

Stress is constantly present in our lives, because there are always, at least, *a)* minor daily hassles that are stressful, *b)* past situations that have been stressful and have left sequelae, or *c)* anticipation that future events will be stressful. Thus, it is important to develop a positive attitude to get us through rough times. A positive attitude consists of both little and big components. Grand wishes or magnificent dreams can pull us through the roughest of times, but this may not be enough. Small positive efforts, ideas, and approaches are needed to pave the way, as well, and they add up. For example, when we need help, a positive nod, a smile, a laugh, and kind words offered by an acquaintance can help. Or, when others need help, support offered by ourselves can help. These efforts act to moderate stress, to put it in perspective, and to open different avenues. That is, when we are determined to maintain a positive attitude despite stress and to maintain basic civility and decency in our dealings with people despite stress, we may break a vicious circle that stress could induce, and, instead, we may end up creating a better mood for all concerned. Small things also consist of using learned ways of destressing, such as breathing techniques, visualization, meditation, and muscle relaxation exercises.

We have two sides to us as we face the stresses around us, even though we may not acknowledge it. We all know that we have the side that feels overwhelmed but, at the same time, we should recognize that, even if it is just a small part of us in the beginning, there is a side that is trying to cope, to organize our resources, and to resolve the problems or situations that confront us. This side is helping us in determining options, seeking solutions, and calculating possible outcomes. We all have a resilient side. Perhaps in moments of difficult stress, that side may be buried and seem lost or incapable of functioning, but it is still there. We have to work to uncover it and bring it back to the surface. **No matter in what situation we find ourselves, the resilient side may be the core kernel of our response to stress and we must keep seeking it.** That is, in each of us, no matter how dark it seems, there is not simply an attitude of resignation to stress but, also, an attitude of hope for recovery. Moreover, as we confront stress, we should always hope to learn from it, if we find ourselves in situations where we cannot master it.

We can come to tip the balance toward the positive, recovery side of our reaction to stress. We can even learn to deal effectively with stress before it arrives in our lives, through appropriate daily stress-reduction exercises and through appropriate daily actions and attitudes aimed at enhancing the quality of life. **Just as our body has an immune system, so does our mind.** Moreover, the number one antibody in this drama between the "bad guy" (stress) and the "good guy" (resilience) is our self, or our will (wanting to beat or accommodate to stress). We are our own psychological antibody.

Bad habits are not born in us. They are created in us by circumstance and by things that happen to us—they are learned. Thus, they can be unlearned. Moreover, we are the best teacher for unlearning our bad habits. We did not choose to have bad habits. They appeared because of things outside of us. But we can choose to replace them. A good way of doing this is by creating good habits that take their place and lead us to better outcomes.

Our core self is still there even when bad habits are present. It may be hidden by the stresses that caused them, and the bad habits that resulted. There is no reason why we cannot be victorious in our battle with stress. Note that by victory, I do not necessarily mean that there is a war against stress and bad habits, and they have to be eradicated. Victory also means learning to control stress and bad habits, learning to co-exist with them, learning to live with them, and learning to live well despite them and be oneself. This is the best victory possible, because it means that when the next stress and bad habit comes along, we will be better able to handle the situation.

Often, I ask clients to recall some pleasant scenes of childhood, the laughter they once knew. Children display not only laughter and smiling when they are having fun but, also, open their mouth wide as if to laugh, such as during rough and tumble play. The function of childhood is to play. Each of us can recall such scenes of total engrossment in the moment. A good suggestion is to share memories of your childhood while on a walk in the park with a friend. Is the vegetation as verdant as that of the neighbourhood park of your childhood? Do you see the rich colouring and delicate shapes of the flowers? Do you hear the wondrous array of vibrant songs of the park birds? Can you feel the soft, caressing breeze of the day? Can you smell with deep breaths the fragrant scents of the roses? Do you notice the busy flight of foraging honey-bees? Do you spy the refined webs of the master weavers, the orb spiders?

There are natural highs that we can experience that are unforgettable. More-over, our brain is equipped with natural pleasure centers, biochemicals that bring pleasure, and drug-free pain-killing mol-ecules. Our body is not only a temple deserving respect but, also, it is a bank of biological wisdom filled with prod-ucts of millions of years of evolution that cannot be obtained either over or under the counter.

An inner calm allows us to remain focused and determined, and brings other rewards. By seeking out our natural inner calm in natural ways, daily living becomes more enjoyable. For example, instead of having an easily activated chip on our shoulder, more likely, a sense of peace and contentment imbues us when we have this attitude. Ad-ditionally, this kind of peaceful attitude is attractive to others, at least when compared to an attitude having aggres-sive elements. People are more likely to gravitate to and favour an individual who is calm and wholly present. The attraction felt by people toward such calm individuals inevitably creates opportunities for them, leading to both personal and work satisfaction. In this way, an attitude of being calm is self-reinforcing, bringing calming and bene-ficial experiences to its practitioner. Calm begets calm, and brings advantages.

Some people deal with stress better that others; they show a calmer attitude, keep their smile, and remain communicative. Partly, they perceive stress differently than others and, partly, they can channel it better. But, also, they have learned that no matter what attitude they adopt, whether positive or negative, the stress is the same. Thus, they have learned that when they are stressed, given the choice between being more negative or more positive, there are benefits in being more positive. It becomes easier for them to think clearly and to get the help of other people. In the end, because they have a more positive attitude when confronted by stress, compared to other people they clear up the source of the stress earlier and easier.

This book has been influenced by another book that I wrote, entitled, *Adult Development, Therapy, and Culture* (1997). That book suggested that human psychology is a continual, ever-changing growth process throughout the lifespan from birth through the elderly period. Thus, the book presents a psychology of hope, change, and adaptation. Therefore, following this tradition, in their therapy, clients and I work together to learn to tell more positive stories about their stress and how they can handle it. For example, I work together with clients to find in the stories that they tell to themselves about themselves even some minor positive signs. As sessions proceed, a new story is built around clients' increasing coping skills, problem solving, and psychological growth. At the heart of each of us are positive qualities, but, because of stress, bad habits are generated that may encircle us and overwhelm our coping mechanisms and resources. However, with appropriate social support (including from mental health professionals, if necessary) and our own inner resources, we can begin to develop alternate and better ways of behaving, allowing us to move forward to control our stress and any bad habits that it had caused us to develop.

I have labelled this type of therapy "transition" therapy, because, no matter what our age, we are all capable of learning to tell more constructive stories to ourselves about ourselves and, thus, growing psychologically. Clients should not consider therapists to be problem solvers and mood changers. Rather, therapists should be thought of as facilitators of one's own abilities to solve problems and change moods. **Each of us has an unending growth potential waiting to be activated.** The therapist's role is to get the ball rolling, and the best way to do this is to get clients to roll the ball themselves.

In this book of essays, I explore further the topics of psychology, stress, destressing, and regaining joy. The first part of the essays consists of 10 sections on fundamental concepts in psychology, often providing definitions. I add, in particular, an essay on rehabilitation, also in 10 sections. The second part consists of a collection of short works dealing with various topics that can help accomplish these objectives. Also, they present a 25-step model of development and its implications, described in my 1997 and 2011 books. Key themes in these essays relate to our growth imperative and our sense of responsibility.

VOLUME II — INTRODUCTION TO DESTRESSING

Each stressful experience need not be an overpowering or overwhelming one, but could be an occasion to learn how to deal better with stress. We can be preventative in our confrontation with stress, and do things beforehand as part of our everyday routine to help us deal better with it. The techniques described in this book are easy to learn and master. They can help us get through many stressful situations that we may face in our lives. We all have grown up with stress throughout our lives, and many times we have dealt with it effectively. For many typical stresses that we encounter in our daily lives, we have developed basic problem-solving skills, have basic coping mechanisms, and know people to turn to for help (family, friends, or other supports in the community). Often, we have dealt with daily stresses successfully and we go on with our lives.

At other times, these stresses are too much for us to handle or, at least, they seem that way to us. Or, a stress comes along that feels like it is the last straw on the camel's back. It can send us over the edge and we lose control. We become anxious, depressed, irritable, and fearful. Our thoughts become full of negative ideas, become pessimistic, and turn catastrophic, as we think the worst. Our bodies tremble and shake, our hearts beat faster, and our breathing gets out of kilter or becomes laboured. We do not know what to do. The stresses build, vicious circles develop, and our world seems like it is falling apart. In moments like these, it is normal to forget that in the past we have dealt positively with stresses, have adapted, and we can do so again.

Sometimes, stress is of our own making, and not from the outside. Ulcers and other related illnesses are pandemic not only because of difficulties that people experience in their daily lives but, also, because of their perceptions that, despite relatively good things happening, they are not perfect or have not turned out exactly right.

For some people, the stresses that they experience are too difficult to face, because they are enormous by anyone's standards. This book speaks to handling stress even when it is most difficult. Stress occurs in varying degrees; however, destressing or countering stress can take place in varying degrees, as well!

One of the goals of the book is to remind us of the basic and effective relaxation and stress management techniques that we can use in our everyday lives. The more we can relax, perform pleasurable activities, distract ourselves, and break the vicious circle of unremitting stress, no matter where we are, the more we can remain in charge of stress and continue to adapt to the difficulties of modern life.

When clients visit my office in order to deal with their problems and stresses, our therapy involves a shared therapeutic conversation along these lines. During these conversations, I try to motivate clients to tell themselves a more positive story about their stress-handling skills, their ability to solve problems, and their ability to see and to follow options.

At the same time, I have them realize that each of us is an individual. We live in particular contexts (specific in place, people, time, and responsibilities), with particular backgrounds and histories, with particular problems and stresses, and with particular personalities and idiosyncrasies. In this book, even though I describe destressing techniques that are applicable to many people, we must always remember to value our individual difference and that of others. There is no one best destressing technique—one size does not fit all. Throughout our lives, we have to seek out new ways to deal with our stresses, ones that work especially for us, and that lead us to more resilience, better coping, and better personal and social growth.

VOLUME III — EMOTIONS INTRODUCTION

In this book, I explore some of the basic emotions that are part of human life. I focus on how these emotions manifest themselves in stressful situations, how to deal with them, and how to make the best of them, so that the stresses that have produced them are dealt with more effectively.

Let's use the metaphor of a drive in nature to explore the various emotions. The shoreline weaves around the cape over tumultuous foothills plunging to the sea, but the driver follows the route hugging the shoreline, admiring the beauty of the landscape. There is a brief frustration at a detour on the road, but it melts into a resolve to continue on and appreciate the view and nature's restive scenery. There is a brief sadness at a bleak, boring part of the road, but it picks up at the sight of beautiful idyllic islands basking in the soft sun of a blue-green inlet. Whenever sadness appears, it is refocused into fond memories that inspire new hopes of finding more such scenes around upcoming bends. There is a brief worry about thunderclouds on the horizon, but instead of imagining the worst, we feel as peaceful as when the dawn or dusk nestles into the natural course of the day. There is brief fear at a close call in the traffic on the road, but it transforms into more careful driving, and the reverie of the trip continues. The predominant emotions are ones of tranquil joy, serenity at the majesty of nature's craft, and wonder about what we shall see next.

When people are exposed to stress, they react with individual variation in emotions, and of course they might manifest a range of negative ones. Some people will show their frustrations more easily, other people will show their sadness more easily, and so on. These variations add to the complexity of understanding emotions. There are no simple rules for understanding which situations produce which emotions. Moreover, when excess stress is added to the life of individuals, the normal rules of emotional expression and control no longer apply. Core negative emotions are more likely to be manifested.

Part of what we have to learn is that at all times our negative emotions lie under the surface. They can be expressed if we become too stressed, even if our family or culture had taught us rules of control for emotional displays. However, negative emotions are not necessarily negative for us. Negative emotions are there to help us know that there is a stressful, problematic situation. Once we know this, we should begin seeking a solution, taking us beyond the negative emotions that the stress activated.

That is, a major purpose of emotions is to help us find the right solution for our problems; that is thy are not meant to stay with us but to have us return to our better feelings through actions that they generate in us. Often, it is normal that stress activates negative emotions, but it is also normal that we act to get the stress that caused them and the emotions themselves under control.

Emotions need to be our guides, not our masters. For emotions to be good guides, we need to review the situation that induced them, reduce the emotional feelings once they are activated, and restructure or canalize these emotions into a new direction and a new perspective. For example, anger is a sign of determination that should lead us to constructive actions that free us of it. **Emotions are there to serve us, not enslave us.**

Emotions have become part of the human repertoire not because of their destructive nature when they get out of control, but because of their constructive nature when they are integrated into part of our successful adaptation to daily situations and stresses. The map of our emotions should look like an ever-changing and adapting shoreline instead of a continuous negative line. Emotions should be quickly oriented to the goal they are meant to serve, and then transformed into adaptive action. Anger should become determination and the frustrating situation should be tackled. Sadness should become a call to refocus and we should adapt to the loss or disappointment underlying it. Worry should become positive anticipation or optimism instead of catastrophic thought or pessimism. Fear should channel us toward mobilization of personal and other resources to deal with the threatening situation that is causing it.

Emotions help define who we are, both in terms of the nature of our individuality and the nature of our species. The more we can act to control and channel negative emotions when they build up or are not redirected appropriately, the more we can free ourselves of their pernicious effects. When they lurk behind every moment, they can seep into our daily lives for the smallest of reasons and become quite strongly expressed, even when not called for. We need to learn to deal with both inappropriate negative reactions in moments of stress and chronic negative emotions that may appear even when there is no stress. By learning how to manage well our emotions, we integrate the best that they have to offer.

VOLUME IV — INTRODUCTION TO DAILY LIVING

The present book deals with issues that arise in our daily lives. First, there is a chapter on the self but, inevitably, as well, the chapter deals with others. The next five chapters concern the basics of family life. These chapters deal with communication, children, and teenagers. Together, the chapters deal with issues that may arise with one's partner and one's offspring. Next, chapter applicable to work follows. Later chapters concern more advanced topics, such as change and inspiration. The last chapter examines major perspectives in psychology, especially the biopsychosocial model, which understands behaviour as complex and the result of interacting systems.

This book might appear to be a smorgasbord of diverse topics, but there is one central theme in them—by learning to destress and to deal with our emotions, we can pass through the problems, issues, and crises of life with our head held high and our family held together.

Life forms a complex system of interacting parts and actors inhabiting a vibrant and ever-changing context. It can appear so overwhelming, when we get caught up in the large forces of stress that daily life may bring. There are dangerous undercurrents that sometimes we do not realize are present, and sometimes enormous problems for which we need solutions. Buffeted by too much stress, perhaps we cannot imagine stabilizing our lives. However, eventually, we act on the stress, and our lives can once more become tranquil and our mind becomes more at ease. We persist in regaining joy and navigating well through the other stresses.

Moreover, in the stresses about us, when we keep as calm as we can in the middle of the turbulence, somehow our calm may influence others with us. Sometimes our serenity and our will to destress provide a good role model that acts on the exterior, facilitating others' success in dealing with stresses encountered.

A major goal of the book is to help us not only deal with stress and emotions that are experienced on the inside but, also, to better adapt to the social and other contexts in out daily life on the outside. The book may help the reader to better achieve these goals. Moreover, it provides material that may help readers develop towards increased psychological change, growth, and flourishing.

VOLUME V — ART INTRODUCTION

The book is about art and nature. The reader will find the art is generally quite simple, consisting of line diagrams. Lines take meaning in context, and the simplest of lines can reveal love, hope, spirituality, and future. The artwork is meant to inspire both relaxation and reflection. The themes explored in the art mostly concern nature and people. This is a good combination, because both communication amongst ourselves and communion with nature are the best healers, and as a society we have an obligation to heal nature.

VOLUME VI — INTRODUCTION
TO THE BEST OF REJOINING JOY

The goals of "Rejoining Joy" and of "Destressing" tap fundamental properties that are part of our human heritage, but often the means of arriving at these goals are difficult to find and, therefore, the goals remain difficult to achieve. In this book, on the topic of rejoining joy and destressing, I present the best of the material in the book series.

Why this book series is unique and compelling

FIRST. This book series is about our capacity to destress, help ourselves heal, regain joy, grow, and live our daily life in harmony. It has a unique format. Three middle books (Books II–IV) in the book series are built around about 500 therapeutic visual figures that I have constructed in session with clients. There is an associated brief text that was written write for each figure. Therefore, each figure-text combination can stand alone. I have put them in a certain order, according to chapter themes, but they do not have to be read in order. The book of essays are in standard format; some are meant to educate/teach and others to inspire/motivate. The art consists of my line drawings, done simply and on relaxing themes. There are relaxing nature photos, as well. I made recordings of my relaxation discourses with clients right in session, and a CD is being made. In these regards, the book

series is multimedia in the service of helping the reader deal with stress and regain joy. Finally, I have written a workbook of exercises to accompany the three books of therapeutic visualizations. These exercises have their own introductions, so the workbook can be read by itself, without reference to the other books.

To summarize, this book series is built on format innovations, especially in its use of therapeutic visualizations. These innovations help highlight the book series' message that we can learn destressing techniques that help us deal effectively with stress, regain joy, and grow psychologically.

SECOND. This book series includes many motivational, educational, relaxation, or healing sayings. Generally, these sayings are short sentences having meaning, humor, or reflection-inducing qualities. I have written about 2,000 of these sayings and have placed them in the margins. Also, in the books, I have bolded one sentence for the text of each figure that has these properties (motivation, education, destressing, healing, etc.). Therefore, every page of the books has material that can stand alone as items for reflection, either placed in the margins or embedded in the text paragraphs. The essay book and art book also have some text and sayings. Overall, my approach is to have multiple pathways to help in healing and in Rejoining Joy. The reader will find different modalities and a continuous stream of short written clips, visual images, and so on, meant to inspire and motivate.

To summarize, this book series includes an easy-to-grasp writing style, with short text written for each of the many therapeutic figures and with sayings placed in the margins. The sayings helping to motivate, educate, relax, and heal, thereby facilitating destressing and Rejoining Joy. The essay portion of the book series consists of many smaller ones, which helps in the reading.

THIRD. The book series is aimed at helping people deal with and overcome stress, whether in terms of major trauma or the daily hassles of life. In this sense, it is attractive to many readers, and can help improve quality of destressing, of mood, and of daily functioning across a range of domains. It teaches techniques in simple ways, from the cognitive-behavioral perspective. At the same time, it reflects wider narrative and systems perspectives aimed at increasing the quality of the stories that we tell ourselves as we confront stress and the problems of daily living. The book series consists of many pages, but its message of having hope, and of learning how to improve one's quality of life, stands out on most every page.

To summarize, a lot of what we do in our daily lives reflect bad habits that we have learned or the lack of knowledge of how to create good habits. This book educates and inspires along these lines, so readers can take charge of their

lives. They can learn how to be who they want to become and learn how to integrate in where they want to belong.

FOURTH. For the most part, I have tried to keep the writing in the books simple and the techniques that I use in my therapy simple. The book series took 15 years to write because it involves about 500 diagrams made with clients in session, aside from the text for the diagrams and other essays that were written. It is a product of my meeting with people in distress so that they can emerge with renewed hope and happiness, confident that they have new tools, new habits, and a new future. Good psychotherapy is not mysterious, because often it uses many of the common psychological procedures that we all use. However, psychologists know how to package them systematically according to contemporary theory, and we know how to teach them well.

To summarize, I have worked to come up with usable and practical techniques and ways of improving oneself and one's relationship with others. I have written motivational and inspirational material that facilitates change from within, self-growth, tranquility, presence of being, and full participation in life.

FIFTH. The second book in the series present essays, and these are mostly educational, although some are reflective, motivational, or inspirational. The first two essays are the most important. They set the scientific stage for the book series. The first essay explains psychology from the perspective of the book series. It introduces critical concepts and key models in psychology. It defines many terms that appear in the ensuing books. Rather than having a glossary of terms after each chapter in the remaining books, I included these terms in the essays. This helps avoid cumbersome footnotes and endnotes, too. The essay on psychotherapy is critical to the book. It is based on an article that I wrote for the journal Psychological Injury and Law in 2008. It is based on 10 areas at which psychotherapy should be targeted in the individual, aside from the possible need for family therapy and other interventions. The second portion of the essays includes ones on a model of development that I presented in a 1997 book that I wrote. This model emphasizes a cognitive developmental model of five stages in development over the lifespan, and it presents affective stages in development acquired in coordination with them.

SIXTH. The sixth book in the series presents my line drawings and, generally, they are relaxing. Many of the drawings have a nature, environmental, or "green" theme. For the first chapter in the book, I added short paragraphs for each drawing. They underscore our connection with nature, and the vulnerability of the planet, animals, and plants, and the need for us to protect them. An additional message of the drawings is that art is easy to do, and any one at any age can do it. The drawings are simple, and often consist of one continuous line. I emphasized movement, as well, for example in drawings of dancing flowers and dancing people. Some of the art is motivational, inspirational, or spiritual, such as some of those drawn on a visit to the holy land.

SEVENTH. The exercise workbook that I have written to accompany the book series on Rejoining Joy is particularly unique. Due to the self-explanatory introductions that accompany each exercise in the workbook it can be read in conjunction with the other books in the book series or it can be read by itself. The exercises in the workbook are meant to be educational and motivational. Often, readers are asked to list their positive attributes or psychological strengths, how they can become more positive, or how they have handled well, or can handle better, a negative among their psychological characteristics and strengths.

To summarize, the book of workbook exercises that I have written present a useful summary of the main points of the book series through the introductory paragraphs preceding each exercise. The items that follow the introductory comments are written in a way to be motivational, and the reader can look forward to being both educated and inspired by this book.

VOLUME VII — INTRODUCTION FOR WORKBOOK

This book is comprised of exercises for the reader to complete. For each of 30 chapters, I have constructed six exercises. Each exercise asks the reader to list up to five items that respond to the exercise. To complete any one exercise, the reader might find that listing one to a few items of the five that are possible to list is sufficient. Some of the exercises request lists of positive core attributes, others request the listing of stresses or negative psychological characteristics that we might have, and yet others ask for ways of resolving or dealing with them. Many of the exercises ask readers to relate or remind themselves of specific techniques, procedures, or ideas learned in the particular chapter that corresponds to the exercises.

One way of learning and applying the meanings and messages of the book series is by reading attentively its contents and using them in responding to the exercises. Another way is to reflect on the particular wording of the exercises as one prepares to fill in the brief lists related to them. In general, in one way or another, each of the exercises emphasizes our core positive psychological characteristics, attributes, or strengths and how we can build them. By thinking about and putting in writing lists of our core positive psychological characteristics, attributes, or strengths and how we can improve them, it is more likely that we will begin the process of accomplishing this objective. The goal of the exercises in the workbook is to help the reader put into practice and function toward achieving the book series's suggested positive paths and goals. **When life becomes knowing, life becomes growing.**

Each exercise in the workbook includes ample space to list the up to five items requested in each exercise. However, the reader should consider leaving blank the spaces provided for responses to the exercises. By keeping a notebook of responses to the exercises in the workbook and avoiding to write directly in the spaces provided, the reader will always have a clean copy of the exercises for future consideration. In this manner, the reader will be able to chart any changes in time in the responses given to the exercises. Indeed, by using a notebook, one will be able to fill in the responses to the exercises every few years so that a chart of one's self-help progress can be made.

Readers may find the exercise workbook most informative and inspiring, and want to share the book with friends and family. Therefore, by creating a separate notebook for oneself, the workbook remains available for others to use. It may be interesting for two people to share their responses, such as two partners in a couple, or two good friends. Those who share their notebook responses with other people may find the responses filled in both informative and valuable.

Both the book series and the workbook exercises from which they are derived have been formulated in simple language, and introductory material is provided for each exercise in the workbook. Therefore, after reading and absorbing the introductions to the exercises, or after consulting the full book series on *Rejoining Joy*, the reader may not even want to fill in by writing the responses to the exercises. Contemplation of the exercises may be sufficient to accomplish their goals of facilitating psychological self-help in readers.

Note that some of the workbook exercises seem to overlap in the items requested. However, sometimes the exercises are similar because one set of items in an exercise ask the reader to deal with a particular area in their psychology in a more general way and another set may require more specific responses. Or, one exercise may deal with one aspect of an area and another may deal with another. Or, sometimes my strategy in writing similar exercises was to have the reader contemplate the same or similar issues in different ways. Finally, some overlap helps reinforce the themes behind the exercises.

These workbook exercises constitue the seventh book in the psychological self-help book series on *Rejoining Joy*. The exercises are meant to both summarize the major themes in the book series and have readers integrate into their psychology these major themes through the responses that they offer in response to the exercises.

Each reader will answer these workbook exercises in her or his unique way. There is no correct answer for any one exercise. Each reader will respond differently and each answer will be valued for what it is, that is, as a statement of where one stands in the present and how one expects to change for the positive psychologically in the future.

In terms of my approach to writing the workbook as the final book in the self-help book series, I hoped that it would lead to a dialogue with the reader. Through its dialogue, the workbook is meant to inspire in readers growth pathways and constructive psychological change.

Before proceeding to the exercises that were written for each of the 30 chapters in Books II–IV of the self-help book series on *Rejoining Joy*, the reader should fill in the following introductory exercises. They have been written to illustrate the major themes of the book series, providing an introduction to the exercises that follow.

VOLUME VIII — INTRODUCTION TO
SAYINGS FOR LIVING, LEARNING, AND LOVING

A saying is an adage, or sentence that can stand alone, and it is meant to offer good advice, or capture a psychological or social reality. Sayings can be found for most anything, and often for any one stand that a saying takes an opposite one can be found. For example, does haste always make waste, or should we be careful at times in not going to quickly, not starting right away, and so on? As I constructed the sayings, I was careful in my wording, so that I did not give facile advice, or try to be wise yet appear too simplistic.

Some of the sayings are repetitive in theme, but that is inevitable. I decided not to cut them down because of this, for different ones will appeal to different individuals. Each of us is unique despite our commonalities, through the different combinations of our characteristics and how they were formed. Moreover, the repetition of sayings on similar themes reinforces their importance.

Note that I created every single saying in the book. Most books of saying are about religious or spiritual themes, or they are taken from famous figures. Often, I had to find succinct and inspiring ways to express the major themes in the book without recourse to existing sayings on these topics, because they are not the typical topics of sayings. Nevertheless, many of the sayings are comparable to sayings expressed by famous people, and the reader may be similarly inspired.

I chose the subtitle of the book of sayings to reflect the major areas of life treated in the book. The book refers to stress, accidents, emotions, daily living, regaining joy, positivity, destressing, managing stress, empowering the core, dealing with a host of daily issues, improving our ways of living, and so on. However, by focusing on the three terms of *Living, Learning, and Loving*, the title captures the main areas of human activity and what we have to do to cope with stress, and flourish rather than just survive. No matter our daily context, we want to adapt well and function effectively, without stress getting in the way. This applies to the worlds of study, work, dealing with people, love, and raising a family. The reader will find numerous sayings in each of these areas.

The approach of the chapters in the *Rejoining Joy* book series does not simply ask us to be more positive, happy, or better. Rather, it shows the reader how to accomplish these and related goals in a realistic manner. It does not simply give the reader positive statements about the self to learn. Rather, it helps facilitate the reader in learning new ways of living by dealing better with the negatives and increasing the positives. In my clinical work, I encourage people to tell better stories about themselves, to find inner qualities and strengths, to learn destressing skills in order to add to them, and to use appropriately these qualities and strengths in solving problems.

FOREWORD

Polly, an adolescent, wrote the following, which is inscribed on her tombstone. I have tried to be as wise:

"Please take care of all those who are good. All the lovers and children. The friends and our families. The poor and the rich. The happy and the sad. Take care of all but those who bring pain and sorrow into the lives of all those who are good. Love the good unconditionally, and that is how you will be loved. Bring joy into the lives of those who lack it. Bring wisdom to those whose eyes need to be opened. Bring love to those who need to be loved: All. For your imperfections are forgiven and all that we have is thanks to you. Protect and love every-one regardless of religion. There is only one true supreme being for us all. For we are all brothers and sisters. End hate, end bad, end wars, end conflicts; while we try to end all things that are bad we forget to enjoy all things that are good. Help us to enjoy life. That is all one needs to be happy:"

I love, I hope, I pray

Polly K.
August 1998

DESTRESSING

When we decide to take control,
stress cannot take advantage.

❧

Even Stress laughs at humor.

❧

Smiles open the doors that stress close.

❧

When we grow, stress does not.

❧

By responding to stress with heightened calm,
we lower its levels.

When two people deal with stress,
it is half as much.

To raise your stress IQ, investigate the problem
and question all solutions.

Half the battle in dealing with stress is starting.

Stress is tone deaf, cannot keep a tune,
and hates music. Play on.

Give stress a facial — smile.

Helping oneself and getting help from
others helps manage worry.

Meditation is effective medication.

When stress makes you sick — send it to the hospital.

Introduce fears to your friends —
breathing exercises, visualizations,
self-talk, and muscle relaxation.

A fast heart needs a slow breath.

The worst enemy of overwhelming stress
is overwhelming preparation.

Stress can be bridged when our inner and
outer connections pass over it.

Stress provides the barriers — we provide the detours.

Fear rescinds its control over us
when we assert our control over it.

Stress is controlled when we put it on hold.

We can learn to be better masters of stress by
learning to perceive better what matters in stress.

꧁

The secret in dealing with stress is to know that
we have secret strengths to help us deal with it.

꧁

Stress is a poor loser —
when we enrichen our resilience.

INCREASING
POSITIVES

Optimism is an acquired habit that is non-addictive,
requires small doses to be effective,
and costs very little per day.

❧

Stopping to think leads to options to act.

❧

Seeing the past as something to learn from,
not live in, can alter the present.

❧

Stress is as big as you believe it — so believe in yourself.

❧

Doing the right thing include stopping the wrong thing.

For every negative thought,
we can find a positive thought.

For every negative thought,
we can find a positive thought.

Bad habits are base camps for scaling positive heights.

Sadness can be a transition point
to a greater serenity.

By doing the right thing, we become the right being.

Fear will take a step back —
when we come to the front.

9

By seeing the whole,
anger has no part.

❧

Drinking less leads to living more.

❧

To conquer bad habits,
make friends with good ones.

❧

Learning to relax helps learning.

❧

Self-doubt is Self-growth.

A smile is worth a thousand swords.

Being open to change opens being.

The challenge of stress is not to recede before it,
but not to lead in front of it.

When optimism becomes a way of life,
we develop a way with life.

Optimism is atomic –
a little goes a long way.

There is little room for feeling down when
we perceive that the only direction is up.

❧

The positive part of us as we deal with pain
can be discovered and can grow to become
more than the pain can ever be.

❧

When we let the more peaceful parts
of ourselves speak, there is less space
for anger to have its word.

❧

From negative story lines that we might tell
about ourselves, there are subplots hinting at the
more positive stories that can be written.

12

Inner beauty has no weight.

❧

Writing new stories about ourselves is never easy,
but living someone else's story, or living an old story
that we have previously told about ourselves,
but that should be changed, is much harder.

❧

When we choose to write positive
stories about ourselves, life may write
positive stories about us.

❧

When we write words about the future
marked by being positive in the moment,
even the story of the past is rewritten.

REDUCING
NEGATIVES

When we decide to change bad habits,
the good times begin.

Stress relinquishes its hold —
when we extinguish our fear.

Stress has the bad habit of going on vacation —
once we trip it up.

Worrying too much accomplishes too little.

Anger is a bad habit waiting for a good replacement.

15

When worry is only wondering,
it encourages rather than discourages.

There are things that we can do to control pain —
and medicine might be low on the list.

When anger is first, we are last.

Anger does not stop the problem,
but it does stop people from solving it.

Bad habits can win only when we play by their rules.

Give anger an expiry date instead
of an extended warranty.

❧

Facing bad habits is a good one.

❧

Life is not fair – when we do not try our best.

❧

Self-definition is not a sentence
but a novel that we write lifelong.

❧

Clearcut bad habits, not mountains.

When worry becomes more stressful
than the stresses to which it is targeted,
it is time to reduce it.

🍃

When pain gets in the way,
we can still find our way.

🍃

By seeing anger as a bad habit
outside of our core, we can more readily
turn to good habits within our core.

🍃

By making negative thoughts short and sweet,
they won't turn sour.

Give negative thoughts a send-off party
instead of a house warming party.

❧

Ask doom and gloom over—and out.

❧

A negative finding its way in is an
invitation for us to help it get out.

WAYS OF
LIVING

Sometimes, nothing is farther from the truth
than what appears closest to reality.

Use a tried and true message — try the truth.

To get on the road to recovery,
start to drive.

Tomorrow is another way.

Self-construction builds with others,
not on them.

Choices are easy to find.
Choosing good ones is easy to delay.

❧

Recognize the hero of your ways.

❧

We may be able to fool some of our selves
some of the time, but we can never fool
even one of ourselves for all time.

❧

We have many selves but one maestro.

❧

Getting thanks gives the most pleasure.

A warm regard is a best reward.

When workers work in teams,
teams team with work.

To change your mind – mind your change.

Chance change to change chance.

Those who pretend to know try to
influence us under false pretenses.

Choices make you think.
Thinking makes choices.

⁕

When we fill our lives with what really matters,
stress does not seem to matter.

⁕

By doing all the small things right,
there is little space for doing big things wrong.

⁕

Stress will have left its mark,
but there is no reason why it cannot
become a mark of courage.

Walking round the block gives direction to the mind.

When we begin to build the self,
we begin to take control of the body.

The past may be written in stone,
but the future is written in imagination.

Valuing the self cannot happen
without valuing the other.

Self-improvement is not an answer but a way.

By making exercising the body a part of our routine,
we escape the routine.

Living the high life is not living life.

EMOTIONS

Laugh a little. Live a lot.

❧

Stress can grow on us, or we can grow from it.

❧

Take the easy way out when confronted
by stress – deal with it.

❧

Stress is in the mind of the beholder.

❧

Bringing mental clarity to the task of perceiving the
complexities that accompany stress simplifies the task
of dealing with the stress with mental clarity.

Stress seems to always go up —
until we get off its roller coaster.

❧

If we are sad because we want to improve our lot,
it is best to start by improving ourselves.

❧

Joy lasts — when we take life seriously.

❧

Acquiring joy is a skill. Socializing is the course.

❧

When moderation controls our extremes,
depression is easier to challenge and master.

Depression is a stepping-stone to
sturdier foundations.

When we stay busy, pain gets exhausted.

When we write our own play, anger has a minor role.

Alcohol is an equal opportunity destroyer.

It is time that we stop broadcasting pain's
story in our lives in order to write our own
script indicating that we can deal with it.

The larger the wound, the larger the healing.

Pain is psychological in part, but its cure
can be psychological in whole.

The choice of how we live our pain is ours, not pain's.

Drinking control begins by acknowledging
that drinking needs control.

Addictions happen when we let them in.
Addictions leave when we decide to ask them out.

COMMUNICATION
VERBAL

When we help someone else solve a problem,
two people learn.

When love has stops and starts, start talking.

Good communication can turn an
argument into an agreement.

Insist on your rights –
and point out his wrongs.

When love has stops and starts, start talking.

Love is a story. We are the words.

Love is a communicable need.

❧

He who listens is heard

❧

May I suggest that masters of communication
suggest rather than dictate.

❧

When decisions are mutual,
both partners are always right.

❧

Sharing words leads to sharing paragraphs.

Talking about talking should be part of talking.

Love has the last word when we share the word.

Give the best of yourself – share what you feel,
what you think, and what you are.

Conquer the great divide – join minds.

Maybe if you told her that maybe she
could say it with a maybe before it, maybe it
will help in the communication.

When communication fills the space
between partners and couple, the distance
between them diminishes.

⤦

To have the evening to yourself,
don't talk to her.

⤦

If you can't tell him like it is,
he will always be like he was.

⤦

Walking skills develop step by step.
Talking skills develop word by word. Social
skills develop person by person. People skills
develop in sharing by sharing with people.

When words are neither here nor there,
you stay there and not here.

❧

Good communication is not like bad golf.
It can get you out of the woods.

❧

When listening is missing,
insisting meets resisting.

❧

If you give listening a chance, both your
minds will travel with the stories heard.
If you give speaking a chance, both your
minds will grow with the stories told.

Presenting argument can be
argumentative or agreeable.

❧

When you learn to love to talk,
her talk will turn to love.

❧

When you want your guy to listen,
tell him in a way that he can hear.

COMMUNICATION
NON-VERBAL

To find an inner joy, boost another's.

When we lend a helping hand,
we are repaid in kind(ness).

We can become sensitized to any little hurt,
or we can become sensitive to the other.

When love includes friendship, it excludes boredom.

"Love" is the most powerful word,
but it is all nonverbal.

"You were meant for me" means —
"I mean to make you happy."

Partners who are friends more
than talk the night away.

Love's challenge — Dare to share.

Lovers are partners in rhyme.

To get more heat in your couple,
turn off the power.

Staying together takes work — and gives fun.

Genuine communication is more
empathy than emphasis.

One kind word can bring
endless communications.

Support offered is growth gained.

A kiss is always with the eyes.

When we hold each other, hurt lets go.

I'll be there for you when you need me.
You being there for me is all I need.

Help is a hold away.

How shall I keep you?
Let me be the ways.

Friends are timeless — when they are there
for good times and bad times.

43

Sticking together glues growth.

❧

The hardest work is the one at home.

❧

We speak with words and
communicate with vibrations.

❧

When couples deal with each other face-to-face,
they end up lips-to-lips.

❧

Sure, women are from Venus and men are from
Mars, but they have to meet on Earth.

RELATIONS

Couples who function as one
become better individuals.

Hot arguments cool passion.

Cheaters get caught – by their conscience.

Men and women are different – until they
share the same values and goals.

When a couple finds the time for each other,
time apart is well spent.

Our love grows the world.

Æ

When we share dreams,
they find ground.

Æ

A kind word is a kind of hurricane.

Æ

To make love work,
we need to work at love.

Æ

When couples share,
commitment grows.

47

We grow to be more than ourselves
through the other.

❧

Soul mates are made — not found.

❧

If you and your partner have a meeting
of minds, other kinds follow.

❧

Meeting half-way could solve it 100%.

❧

Insisting on one-way could leave you single.

To double the fun, make your
communication two-way.

❧

When you are trying to get personal, keep in
mind that gifts cannot replace the person.

❧

Give your social life a battery boost
by seeking new connections.

❧

When you find your feminine in
your masculine or your masculine
in your feminine you might find
someone who is more balanced.

Finding a third-way could triple the agreement.

⌒☙

Finding a long lost friend is like
finding a part of your self.

⌒☙

When you say what you feel and feel what
the other might feel when you say it,
the other might feel what you say and
might say what you need to feel.

LOVE

Couples who never stop going out
on dates never stop dating.

❧

When love rules, neither partner is a monarch.

❧

The best prenuptial agreement: Cherish her honor.

❧

Reach for the top. Then, caress her
hair and soothe her mind.

❧

Honeymoons last — when we
remain shining examples.

The lure of love needs the allure of effort.

❧

Love progresses in stages.
Climb the steps together.

❧

There are so many dimensions to love
when there are no hidden ones.

❧

Love and affection go cheek to cheek.

❧

Love is not an end but a beginning.

Being faithful brings bedded bliss.

Love binds couples like stars bind sky.

Charity begins at home.
Give love to your partner.

Diamonds are forever — when the
fingers keep touching.

Love is the spark for so many flames.

Love is like the alphabet — it can be
put together in a lot of ways.

In couples, a warm shoulder warms the bed.

Love is part passion, part caring,
part sharing, and part dedication.
Do not let it part ways.

Marriage begins after the honeymoon.

Love grows — when each partner is allowed to.

Partners who live in truth,
lie down.

Love's compass always points
above the horizon.

Medicines cure. Love heals.

Love is an epidemic that
needs lots of bed rest.

Love is bind.

A hug to start the day extends
into the evening.

When life pulls us apart,
love keeps us whole.

SUCCESS

The better we ask, the more
questions we have.

The rule is – goals should guide, not rule.

There is no choice but to
keep our options open.

Falling deeper means climbing higher.

Ask others for advice.
Ask yourself for decisions.

When solutions are short-sighted,
problems are all we see.

❧

The farther we look afield, the greater the harvest.

❧

Thinking is a question of asking questions.

❧

Letting others decide your future
is a terrible decision.

❧

Trying is the only thing that
we can always succeed at.

In the realm of the impossible lies many
wasted opportunities.

❧

For every answer, there is a question.
For every question, there are more questions.

❧

We should learn how to find answers
and how to find questions.

❧

Changing is half wanting and half working.

❧

Certainty is the absence of humility.

Determination gets us going;
Enthusiasm keeps us going;
and Effort gets us there.

Dreaming creates possibility.
Working for it creates reality.

It is not what the person has that makes her,
but what the person makes of what she has.

When you are not sure whether things will
work out, you will be joining a lot of successful
people who had thought the same way.

Our goal is not to reach the end but
to extend our reach.

The future holds what we hold up to it.

Frontiers may defy us or define us.

Wish we could do better.
That should be our only wish.

In starlight, worlds look so different.
In vision, they can be.

Horizons pull the sky to their ends.

The future is not written in the past,
or the present, or the future.

Someone who professes to have the
answer does not know the question.

Resolve helps solve.

One thing at a time well done is better
than many parallel blunders.

Problems are solutions waiting to happen.

Times that are trying should be
considered times to keep trying.

When it seems hard to start doing some
things, some start doing things.

If you keep at it, you will get with it.

The journey is not the road
but the direction we give it.

GROWING

The wisdom of sadness is that it is
telling us that something is missing and
that we have to do something about it.

The worst tragedies may lead to
the most profound discoveries.

A loss can be a win for growth.

Seeing beyond the self takes the self beyond.

When we stretch our vision, our actions rebound.

When responsibility is continually renewed,
we are continually new.

❧

There is a down path — and there is
walking down the path.

❧

A turn for the worse is not necessarily the worst turn.

❧

Imagining change is a start to outcomes
that we could not have imagined.

❧

The more we know, the more we new.

It is not so much that we learn to repeat
but that we learn repeatedly.

Figure out your potential. Then, make it more.

The open mind leaves bright shadows.

People grow toward where they aim.

Each person has secret strengths,
unknown gifts, untapped resources, splendid
potentials, and precious possibilities.

Each life can become an epic journey.

❧

Small changes can be, at once, great changes.

❧

A healthy harvest works all
the corners of life's field.

❧

The only part that is innate about
ourselves, that is fixed in our genes, is our
ability to grow, change, and emerge.

❧

Each of us has part of us where other worlds will be.

GROWING

When we learn from each experience,
we seek experiences to learn.

Excluding others blocks one's path.

71

BEING

Joy comes not from what we do
but from whom we are.

Â·â

If joy is the goal, being good is the means.

Â·â

Being free is a question for being.

Â·â

Do not ask what you need for yourself
but what yourself needs to ask.

Â·â

Seeing deep inside brings
us farther outside.

Growth transmitted is self transformed.

Goodness comes from being well bred —
not from being part of a breed.

The brain gives us sight. It also gives us vision.

We are created in the image
that we create for ourselves.

Seeing the truth means acting on it.
Acting on the truth means seeing.

I am only a part of We,
but We is only a part of I.

When we think of what is our I,
it already was.

The human building needs no stones.

Humanity is a sea. Each of us is a wave.

The invisible wealths are the richest.

Each of us is a part of the whole.
The whole is a part of each of us.

Bearing is not bestowed — but sowed

Empathy is sympathy is
sensitivity is responsibility.

Generosity is the opposite of grandiosity.

Goodwill starts with good will.

Compassion should be our passion.

Mercy deserved should be mercy given.

Help should not be what we do to others when called,
but what we do to others before called.

Be unto others as you would
have them be unto you.

We must do more than do unto others.
We must be unto others.

The strength of the fabric lies in the weave,
not in the fiber.

❧

Good in the act or act in the good.

❧

Freedom to be is not only about Me.

❧

Puzzle keepers are never answer keepers.

CIVICS

When we give freely of
our time, time flies.

Freedom is not for the taking.

Responsibility is freedom's reward.

It is not what I do or what I am
but what we do and what we are.

Be kind to yourself – give to another.

True teachings aim to empower,
not enslave.

⚬

Great teachers want you to
know more than them.

⚬

Giving to life endlessly give endless life.

⚬

When we freely give, we greatly get.

⚬

Standing up for one's rights is enabling.
Standing up for someone else's is ennobling.

Conscientiousness is Consciousness.

If decency marks our life,
we will make our mark.

Each of us can make a special difference —
by helping others find their special difference.

To maximize personal growth,
maximize community involvement.

If we do good, we be good.

Some say, some say they do,
some do what they say, some do.

They say that we are all brothers.
The brothers should let the sisters' help realize that.

The best ideas inspire beyond themselves
and encourage the best in people.

The more I give of myself, the more I give to myself.

Facing each other is facing forward.

The only dynasty that lasts is democracy.

Peoples are humans first
and peoples second.

Seeding hope delivers realities.

Liberty should be more than an ideal —
it should govern a way of life that we make ideal.

Their children cannot help yours
if you do not let them be born.

A circle of care is a ring of steel.

Persecution kills – the psyche
of those who persecute.

Charity begins in the home, in the street,
in the shelters, in the...

When we unmake hate, we make ourselves.

SPIRITUAL

When I do not know which
way to turn, I look up.

Joy is not an island beach but an inner harbor.

Sometimes mystery is the only answer.

Light your way with glimmers of hope.

When each moment is precious,
life is golden.

When all faiths accept all faiths,
integrated faith emerges.

❧

Teaching that stops at one book
or tradition stops learning.

❧

Worship – not warship.

❧

One is the biggest number in the universe.

❧

Spirituality is a tree living in our roots.

A high-minded spirit starts with
a high spiritual mind.

❧

Each of us can write new psalms in our own way.

❧

Each holy book is an invitation to write a better one.

❧

Freedom comes from choosing to help
others while having an inner peace.

❧

We have met our maker —
and it is ourselves.

Faith is what we choose to decide.
Fate is what we decide to choose.

❧

Be godly — do everything that is humanly possible.

❧

Reality reaches to the horizon.
Spirituality reaches beyond.

❧

When we pray for more than ourselves,
we become more than ourselves.

❧

The burning bush is a story about our fire.

90

One day, religion will catch up to spirituality.

People in a circle are equally
close to the center.

As we walk through the valleys of hope,
we are our guides.

Accepting mystery enhances discovery.

Transcendence goes only as far
as our kindness allows.

A sense of loss is the messenger
of what is precious in life.

From sounds come words.
From words come universes.

Peace is not a product but a process.

NATURE

Earth — we are all on it together.

They say that the world was created in seven days.
They say that it can be destroyed in one.

If we let animals be, we will be.

Nature needs our nurture.

Wild flowers are signs
of the timelessness.

Do not let the willow weep for what we do.

Hands that help birds hold
human flight aloft.

Nature is the temple.
Planting is the prayer.

Get vision. Watch a flower.

If eagles had tears, they would
cry too much for us.

A midsummer night's dream — no nuclear winter.

Great civilizations leave legacies.
They should leave forests.

Listen to the best music —
be in tune with nature.

A bird in the hand is worth freeing.

The person who can save the planet
lives within each of us.

The earth is a mirror of how we treat it.

Birds are the skies' songs.

Nature asks for one thing in order
that it thrive – respect.

Pollution has a habit of being
recycled in our bodies.

To stay on top of the food chain,
we have to preserve it.

Harmony with nature brings
harmony to the self.

Children who learn nature
find schooling natural.

Become an environmental activist —
hike, climb, run, and breathe deeply.

Think green, choose green, and live green.

Nature has outlasted every uncivilization.

Animals are nature's children.

❧

Nature has existed billions of years —
and we can wipe it out in one.

❧

Do unto nature and you
would have it do unto you.

❧

Humans evolved in nature so
that we can keep it evolving.

LIFE

We power the grip of the day's tasks by
the dreams of the night's hopes.

Each crawl of the caterpillar is a step
toward the butterfly's flight.

Coping is built on skill and will.

Coping is part know how and part asking how.

We can choose to dwell on the past —
or we can choose to dwell in the present.

Coping is problem solving and problem finding.

Passive coping needs active reworking.

If it can go wrong, it will.
If you will to make it better, it can.

Coping is part thinking, part feeling,
and part ourselves.

We should deny neither our pain
nor our capacity to control it.

Taking charges of pain takes away what it thrives on.

Pain can get in the way – only when it gets its way.

The best recipe for pain control includes
two parts medication, two parts psychological
techniques, and ten parts motivation.

Pain begins in the body and finishes in the mind.

The more we control bad temptations,
the more we are free for good ones.

To control fear, send it off on your merry way.

❧

Fear is one part of us. Courage is another.

❧

To get a grip of anger, grab it by its beginnings.

❧

Tragedy is part of life,
except when life creates tragedy.

❧

We have a choice when it comes to anger —
the rewards of its control or the repeated
wars of its expression.

We do not know what the future holds,
but we do know that we hold it in our hands.

☙

By facing change, we encourage stability.

☙

Emotion is the Great Motivator,
but our thoughts should be the Great Finisher.

☙

Accidents have no purpose;
Purpose has no accidents.

☙

Empower yourself – weaken anger.

YOUNG
AT HEART

The brain is the mind's muscle. Keep it fit.

Sleeping at night is easier when we live the day wiser.

There is more common nonsense
than common sense.

Joy can start with a good word or a tender touch.
It never ends with a good word or a tender touch.

Mental gymnastics begins with a
balanced beam on our face.

Grab life by the horns — volunteer to help the needy.

If you know that sometimes the self that you
show is only for show, the show can go on.

Without our heart, we lose our mind.

Healthy foods in the fridge mean
healthy foods in the body.

Life is an obstacle course for some
and a spectacular course for others.

When we write new stories about ourselves
that describe how positive and constructive
that we want to become, even our old selves
will not be able to put down the book.

When others write your story,
fire the writer.

The most important trips are those
between our mind and the moment.

Get a good head on your shoulders —
hug your parents.

Beauty is in the wise of the older.

Dignity is learned and earned.

Time may be the fourth dimension,
but the wisdom in its use is the fifth dimension.

When life becomes lifelong learning
and growing, the only thing in which we
wish to overindulge is life itself.

Humor avoids stupor.

The script of our life is not written in advance, and the director is not chosen without our consultation.

Writing it down lifts us up.

Feeling young is not about one's age but about one's approach to one's age.

Wisdom does not lie in the person but in the engagement of the person in life.

The fountain of youth lies in the fountain of wisdom.

The young have their future in front of them;
the elderly have their future to put
in front of the young.

We are not less than our stories —
and not more than our imagination.

CHILDREN

Love is a medium.
Children are the message.

❧

Embrace your inner self – hug a child.

❧

Be good to yourself – smile to a child.

❧

Children are love's answer.
Love is children's need.

❧

Teenagers are great educators –
they test our limits.

Teens think that curfew is time aplenty.

❧

Teenagers want their own individual styles, clothes, and tastes. So how come they all look the same?

❧

Teenagers are good kids – when they do not want to be adults too fast.

❧

Teenagers are concerned about universal mysteries, or so it seems – everything is WHY?

❧

Children see as high as our eyes look.

Teenagers are curious — they keep
questioning our requests.

To bring out the best in a child,
bring out the best in yourself.

We are the spire to which children aspire.

Babies start saying the way it is before they can talk.

When you tell teenagers the rules
of the house, they stop ruling.

Children go through ages, phases, and stages.
Parents join the ride.

A child talking for himself does
not mean that he must be talking
against the person listening.

The race is between the child curiosity
and the parent's energy.

Babies roll, then crawl, then walk, then talk.
Parents try to supervise and not flop.

Toddler math:
There is no such thing as the
terrible two's. It starts earlier.

Toddler parental math: 24/7, for
25 hours a day, 8 days a week.

First-borns want both exclusive
attention and second-borns.

Play trumps sibling rivalry.

LEARNING

Problem solving begins with problem learning.

❧

To get far in life, stay near the books.

❧

Education begins with the 3 R's at home —
respect, role modeling, and
rewarding good behavior.

❧

Children are very teachable —
when we learn how to teach them.

❧

Nurture your child. Bring him in the garden.

School teaches the letters of the alphabet.
Parents teach the code of living.

❧

Libraries provide children with infinite books.
Books provide children with infinite ideas.

❧

Take the courses that you need to succeed in life —
art, music, social skills, and empathy.

❧

To stand tall, sit before the books.

❧

Learning is half teacher, half you.

Schoolbooks provide working knowledge.

Genes tell us where we grow.
Parents tell us how we grow.
We do the growing.

Seeds start. Parents continue.
School carries on. We carry forward.

Teach the little children — to teach themselves.

Developing a brain is child's play.

Children can be only as great as the educational
system that we build for them.

The more knowledge we have, the
more knowledge we can create.

Children teach us from the day they are born.

The love of learning begins with the
love received in the home.

What the child learns, the adult teaches.

123

Genetic potentials are limit-setting factors, but
love potentials are growth-setting factors.

Give a child a helping hand —
pick out a good book to read.

Learning starts in the womb to the
sounds of the singing voices around,
or the stinging disputes.

PARENTING

Family breeds content.

Raising toddlers should be child's play.

Children respect limits delivered respectfully.

Give children everything they ask for from
the deepest of their hearts — love.

Parents who foster their children's
psychological growth at all turns grow
themselves at all points.

Children need praise, not pennies.

Children do what you do – not what you say.

Giving emotional security to children
secures their future.

When children need to turn to someone,
head straight for them.

Being a good parent is making one
giant step for human kindness.

127

When children can trust our word,
they know what to say.

❧

It is never too late to say that you
are sorry, especially to a child.

❧

Children see what we choose not to show them.

❧

Children love the love and fight the fight.

❧

Hit it off with a child — don't hit.

When the family works together,
the family plays together.

When we hurt a child, we hurt the universe.

When adolescents have good role models,
they influence their future.

For adolescents to look forward to the future,
they need our presence.

The measure of success lies in the look of your child.

Work fills the bank account and family
fills the thank account.

To get a good credit rating, take your
children on an outing.

A child loved is a child launched.

Be a change agent — Give good care to a child.

By helping the child grow in peace,
we help peace grow in the child.

Be fair to your children – praise them all.

❧

Life starts with DNA – Do Not Abuse.

❧

Our families do not deserve our
drinking, they deserve us.

❧

When parents externalize a problem with a label,
it is easier for children to end up internalizing good
habits in conjunction with controlling bad ones.

❧

When you have children, work is rest.

This work is for the reader who desires to learn and grow, to deal with stress, and to handle emotions and daily life. It promotes mindful participation, self-respect, and joy. To see the full range of the works by Dr. Young on rejoining joy, consult the website rejoiningjoy.com.

www.ingramcontent.com/pod-product-compliance
Lightning Source LLC
Chambersburg PA
CBHW060852280326
41934CB00007B/1017